a little book of India

a little book of India

CELEBRATING 75 YEARS OF INDEPENDENCE

Ruskin Bond

PENGUIN
VIKING

An imprint of Penguin Random House

VIKING

USA | Canada | UK | Ireland | Australia
New Zealand | India | South Africa | China

Viking is part of the Penguin Random House group of companies
whose addresses can be found at global.penguinrandomhouse.com

Published by Penguin Random House India Pvt. Ltd
4th Floor, Capital Tower 1, MG Road,
Gurugram 122 002, Haryana, India

Penguin
Random House
India

First published in Viking by Penguin Random House India 2022

10 9 8 7 6 5 4 3 2 1

ISBN 9780670096626

Typeset in Baskerville MT Pro by Manipal Technologies Limited, Manipal
Printed at Thomson Press India Ltd, New Delhi

www.penguin.co.in

*In gratitude to a loving family for seeing me
through a difficult year.*

—R.B.

'Thou brave one, be bold, take courage, be proud that thou art an Indian, and proudly proclaim—"I am an Indian—every Indian is my brother."'

—Swami Vivekananda

A Note From The Author

AS 84 OF MY 87 YEARS have been lived in this, my beloved country, I can feel justified in celebrating 75 years of India's Independence along with millions of my fellow citizens.

This little book does not claim to be a political or historical analysis of events, although I have dwelt on the highlights of the last 75 years of India's progress to maturity as a nation. It is a record of some of my memories and impressions of this unique land—of its rivers and forests, literature and culture, sights, sounds and colours—an amalgamation of the physical and spiritual.

We celebrate our freedom in different ways. I celebrate it with the written word.

Ruskin Bond

INDIA is a land of rivers, and the Ganga is its life blood.

From *Gaumukh* (the Cow's Mouth), high on the Himalayas, down through the pine-scented mountains and valleys, it gathers into itself hundreds of streams and mountain torrents, making its way through the lower ranges until it bursts into full view at Rishikesh and Haridwar and cities downstream.

This mother river winds across the plains of northern India, where sugar cane, paddy, golden mustard are grown by millions to feed and sustain even greater millions. And the people living on its banks feel favoured by the gods and send diyas and flower petals downstream to show their gratitude.

There are many great rives in India. It is a land of rivers. They form the veins and arteries of this ancient land. But Ganga is the mother of them all.

THOSE MOUNTAINS! Himalaya, Himachal, Himaal . . . They form a chain, a protective bracelet, cutting off our peninsular from the windswept deserts of central Asia.

There is more than one way of perceiving the mountains. You can see them as a pilgrim, your destination the sacred shrines of Badrinath, Kedarnath, Gangotri, Yamunotri. In olden times you trudged up from the foothills, climbing from 3,000 ft to 12,000 ft, several days on the footpath, nights spent in wayside inns and dharamshalas. It took more than a week to complete your pilgrimage. It was an epic journey.

Today, there are motor roads that take you most of the way, and within a few hours you can be at the portals of one of the temples.

Every year, when the snows melt, hundreds of thousands of people from all corners of the country undertake the pilgrimage.

SOME, like me, look at the mountains
for their majesty, their verdure, their
permanence, their tremendous solitude.

Men come and go; the mountains remain.

I remember ascending the winding path to Tungnath, the highest temple in the central Himalaya. Within the space of an hour, I had passed from the tree line to a meadow-land to the snow line. A golden eagle watched my lonely progress.

A *runda* (a small rodent looking like the dormouse in *Alice in Wonderland*) popped his head out of the ground, gave me one startled look, and popped back into the security of his burrow.

Up there, sky and mountain were one. I could blend with both, though briefly. The rest of India claimed me too.

HUMBLE, hardy folk live in the mountains, scratch a living from the stony soil. The streams are down in the valleys. The higher your home, the harder your life.

I stood on a hilltop, admiring the sunset, the winterline. My companion belonged to a small village on the lower slopes of this range.

'That sunset,' I said. 'Isn't it beautiful?'

'If you say so,' he said, wishing to please me. 'But you cannot eat sunsets.'

Some go to the hills to admire the view, to feel rejuvenated. Hill people go to the plains to earn a living, their first choice being the Armed Forces. They stand guard over our frontiers, send money home so that the family can buy a new plough and a bullock to pull it.

TREES

This is a land of trees and forests.

Should we start at the tree-line or go down
to the coast for a change?

I have spent most of my life among oak
and deodar, but last year I went down to
the coast, our eastern seaboard, where the
fishing community braves high seas and
cyclonic squalls in order to provide us with
the delicious fish and prawns that make
dining in or out a special experience.

And coconuts, fresh from the tree.

Palm trees don't give much shade, but who would want to sleep beneath a coconut tree? A coconut falling on your head could well despatch you to another world.

Palm trees seldom topple over. They don't try to resist the wind, they bend with the wind, they blend with the elements.

We too must blend with nature, not resist it.

MANGOES ...

Ah, the fruit of the gods.

Hundreds of varieties, growing all over the sub-continent; from the foothills to the coastline.

Children love mangoes. So do grown men and women. So do parrots and other fruit-eating birds. So do monkeys. And fruit-eating beetles.

Some time ago I wrote a little verse:

'If born again

I'd sooner be

A parrot in a mango tree!'

Well, better a parrot than a beetle or a
monkey.

ASSUMING that the mango is our most popular fruit, what would our second most popular fruit be?

The banana, I suppose.

We get bananas most of the year-round, and they are relatively inexpensive.

I have a friend in Kolkata who eats lots of bananas. He has a couple for breakfast, two or three with his lunch, and a banana milkshake for supper. He will soon be celebrating his 100th Birthday, so I suppose that says something for bananas.

One the other hand, it doesn't prove anything. I know another centurion who detests bananas and claims that her longevity is due to her fondness for hilsa fish.

INDIA is a land of rivers.

It is a land of mountains.

It is a land of the sea, for the sea surrounds two-thirds of it.

It is also a land of the desert—the red sands of Rajasthan extend to the sandstone fortresses of Bikaner and Jaisalmer in the west, the glories of Jaipur and Udaipur in the centre, and Ajmer in the south.

Rajasthan, the land of princes, of Rajput glory and chivalry, immortalized in *Tod's Annals of Rajasthan*.

Every state in India, big or small, has more history than any single nation of Europe or America. India was a land of hundreds of former kingdoms, all replete with their own traditions, histories, languages.

Now they are all one. Vallabhbhai Patel, the strong man of India, brought them all together under one canopy, one flag, one free and independent India.

1947 BROUGHT INDEPENDENCE
from colonial rule. The British Empire
had run its course. India was the first
nation to be free. Gandhiji's non-violent
satyagraha approach had worn down the
rulers. Freedom fighters had filled the jails.
There was no longer room for them.

A certain General Dyer, a sadist and a racist, had ordered his soldiers to open fire on a peaceful gathering of thousands in an open ground in Amritsar. Over a thousand were killed or wounded. This wanton and stupid act only accelerated the freedom movement.

By the time World War II had started, an Indian National Army had been formed by the revolutionary, Subhas Chandra Bose. Now Britain was under pressure from two very different Indian leaders. Its economy shattered by the costs of the war, Britain agreed to an early transfer of power.

But there was a price to pay for freedom. Partition.

I WAS a schoolboy, twelve years old, when the Indian flag went up on the flagpole in the playing field of my boarding school in Shimla. Down came the old Union Jack, familiar to us over the years.

There was excitement in the air. A new nation had been born, and we were a part of that birth—some two hundred boys of different faiths and backgrounds. In pouring rain, we marched up to the Mall, to join the parade and listen to speeches by an array of notables. Shimla had been the country's summer capital, and Mountbatten, the Viceroy, was still in residence.

No television in those days, no internet, but Mr Nehru, now Prime Minister, had spoken to the nation over the radio, his speech a reflection of his knowledge of world affairs and his familiarity with the English language.

How we depended on radio in those far-off days—for news, for messages from our leaders, for commentaries on cricket matches played at home and abroad.

Melville de Mellow, our most celebrated news reader and commentator, had been a student of our school. His familiar, booming voice brought us descriptions of parades, celebrations—and disasters.

India had been divided. In their haste to ring the bells of freedom, our leaders had agreed to the partition of Bengal and Punjab on the basis of religion.

A massive displacement of populations had to take place—and did take place, amidst riots, mass killings and human tragedies. West and East Pakistan were created. Millions of Hindus and Sikhs were forced to leave their homes and flee to India; millions of Muslims, fleeing to Pakistan, suffered in much the same way. Murders and reprisals continued for days, weeks, months.

Britain had always described India as the 'Jewel in the Crown'. Now the Jewel had been smashed to pieces. Mountbatten had been under pressure from the British government to hasten the process of Independence, and the result had been terrifying—for a time at least . . .

Our school was divided too, but not from communal strife. One-third of our boys came from homes in Lahore and other cities of what was now Pakistan. The school itself came under threat from violent groups in the bazaar. In the middle of the night, all our Muslim boys were bundled into Army trucks and driven to the borders of their new country. They arrived safely, but I was never to see them again.

When I came home to Dehradun that winter, the worst of the conflict was over. I was thirteen, born in India of British and Anglo-Indian parents. No one ever molested me, not in Delhi, not in Dehra. Now I strolled across our extensive *maidaan*, to one of our cinemas. The film was called *Blossoms in the Dust*.

Ten minutes into the showing of the film there was an interruption, the lights came on, and the manager made an announcement.

'I'm sorry, but we must discontinue the show. We have just received news that Gandhiji has been shot.'

GANDHIJI was no more.

I walked home through a town that was strangely silent. No riots, no slogans on the streets. The country was in shock. The assassin was a man whose strong ideological differences with the views of the Mahatma had driven him to take the life of the man who, more than any other, had been on the forefront of the long march to freedom.

In time, the country recovered from this tragic setback.

India always recovers—from foreign invasions, colonial exploitations, famines and floods, quakes and cyclones, epidemics on a grand scale.

Sometimes it takes time, but India recovers.

The seasons pass, the crops come up, the mangoes ripen, the monsoon comes and goes, the snows melt, the Ganga flows . . .

THE NEHRU years were upon us—a decade in which India strove to find its feet, to banish poverty, to emerge with self-esteem from two hundred years of colonial exploitation.

Big dams came up. New cities expanded. Jamshedpur, Rourkela, Bhubaneshwar, Chandigarh.

In my schooldays there had been no Chandigarh. Now I could watch the city being built. I could be part of history. We were all part of history.

CHANDIGARH

A treeless plain near the foothills became
a hive of activity as shopping centres,
government buildings, residential sectors
came up looking very different from the
buildings in our older cities. A master
architect was at work. Hundreds of trees
of different varieties were planted. In a few
years' time it would be a green city.

To plant a tree is to believe in the future.

I have always enjoyed visiting some of our older cities, appreciating their contrasting styles of architecture—the Jain influence in Ahmedabad, the Hindu influence in Ujjain and other temple cities, the colonial influence in cities like Mumbai, New Delhi; the French influence in Puducherry; the Mughal influence in Lucknow and Agra.

Unfortunately, as many beautiful cities grew, there was little space for parks and gardens.

One exception is Jamshedpur, founded by a great Parsi industrialist, Jamshedji Tata, who gave this industrial city a green and gracious look.

Plant a garden if you believe in tomorrow.

MR NEHRU, INDIA'S first prime minister.

A dapper individual, almost always to be
seen with a red rose in his buttonhole.
He had been to an English public school
and University and spoke and wrote
fluently in English. He was a westernized
Indian, but also a man of the people. He
loved the crowds and addressed them
with enthusiasm. He was impatient of
security and frequently gave a slip to his
bodyguards.

One of them, an ex-bodyguard, who met me around 1960, said: 'I had a hard time keeping up with him. He kept darting off in unexpected directions. I lost weight running after Pandit Nehru'.

When I met this gentleman, he was putting on weight, relieved at having passed on his duties to another bodyguard.

THE NEHRU years were, by and large, peaceful years and placid years with India beginning to make its influence felt in the international arena as a champion of non-alignment.

We were on good terms with both Russia and the U.S.A., and China was looked upon as a special friend.

But in 1959, when China took over Tibet and the Dalai Lama found refuge in India, the relationship changed. Territorial disputes flared up, and Chinese troops swarmed down the passes into North-east India.

They returned to the border after
negotiations with the Indian government,
but the damage had been done and
relations with China were never the same.

Nehru was devastated. He saw the invasion as a breach of trust and a blow to his own pride and self-esteem. It affected his health and probably took a few years off his life. But we remember him with affection, for he was a man of many gifts and achievements, and his literary works—*An Autobiography* and *Discovery of India* (written in jail during the freedom movement) remain with us as monuments to his achievements.

THE NEHRU FAMILY had been
anchored by Jawaharlal's father, Motilal,
a successful barrister. Jawaharlal joined
the freedom movement after completing
his formal education. But his daughter,
Indira, grew up in politics. She handled her
widowed father's affairs, brought up two
children, threw herself into the Quit India
Movement.

She did not immediately succeed her father as Prime Minister, but when she did, it seemed natural and inevitable.

She was a strong leader, and she had no hesitation in sending the Indian Army into East Pakistan and helping to bring about the creation of Bangladesh.

But her premiership was marked by many upheavals—an 'Emergency' of almost two years duration, during which most of her political opponents were imprisoned, along with outspoken critics. She was voted out of office, then back again. The Khalistani movement gained momentum. She sent the Army into the Golden Temple. And she fell to the bullets of her own Sikh bodyguard.

There were reprisals. Thousands of Sikhs lost their lives, in New Delhi and other northern cities. It was a tumultuous period, reminiscent of Partition.

Rajiv Gandhi, Indira's older son, was persuaded to take over the leadership of the nation. He did not have a political background, but he did his best, with the aid of his well-wishers and his supportive wife—until he too fell to an assassin's suicide bomb, the tragic outcome of his efforts to bring about a solution to the civil war in Sri Lanka.

GRADUALLY, other political parties were coming to the fore, in particular the Bharatiya Janta Party (BJP). Its symbol was the lotus, a water lily, always to be seen in the hand of the goddess Lakshmi, as she dispensed prosperity to the faithful.

The rose was fading, the lotus was in full bloom.

A modest, thoughtful man, Atal Bihari Vajpayee, was the BJP's man of the moment.

A few years before he had become Prime Minister, I had seen him walking down Mussoorie's Landour bazaar, accompanied by just one or two companions, chatting to shopkeepers and others without any pretentions or desire for show.

When the BJP came to power, that same modesty, courtesy, and air of deliberation, made him a Prime Minister very different from his predecessors; a man who could, in many ways, identify with the aspirations of the people.

THE EBB AND FLOW of politics, the swing of political fortunes, is natural to a democratic nation.

We have had many outstanding Prime Ministers—Nehru, Shastri, Indira Gandhi, A. B. Vajpayee, Manmohan Singh, many others—and now Narendra Modi, a man of humble beginnings, whose political acumen, natural sagacity, and yogic willpower have brought him to the top and kept him there through two general elections.

A NATION that sings is a happy nation.

Indians love music—religious music, classical music, popular music, folk music, even western music.

When my granddaughter Beena sings during her morning puja, I know it's going to be a good day. When I hear a bhajan I feel rested, in harmony with the world.

In India, we sing during festivals, during harvest time, when the rains are good, when flowers bloom, when rivers run sweetly. We sing for prosperity, for goodwill to all, and for the greater glory of the Creator.

Listen to the birds. They sing so beautifully. We are in good company.

On this day of Independence, 2021, I will keep my window open so that I can hear everyone singing.

AND WHAT do I read today?

Something classical would be appropriate,
I think. Classical, but in some ways
contemporary.

I turn with anticipation to Kalidasa's 5th
century drama, *Shakuntala*, and I am not
disappointed.

For Kalidasa was a poet of nature. His lyrical descriptions of India's flora and fauna bring the play to life. And the heroine herself is half-bird, her name being derived from the *Shakuntalas* or birds with which she so easily converses.

Shakuntala effaces differences of race, culture and language, and speaks to us across the centuries. It is a delight. It is a delight to return to it again and again.

The Mahabharata is a treasury of epic poems and spiritual words, as well as such immortal tales as *Savitri*, or *Love and Death*, one of my own favourites. This spirited Savitri uses all her charm and wiles to persuade Yama, the god of death, to return her husband to the land of the living. The gloomy but good-humoured god gives in to her sweet words.

'Then Savitri arose, and tied her hair,
And lifted up her lord upon his feet;
Who, as he swept the dry leaves from
          his cloth,
Looked on the basket full of fruit.
          "But thou,"
The Princess said, "tomorrow shalt
          bring these;
Hand me thine axe, the axe is good
          to take."
So saying, she hung the basket on a branch,
And in her left hand carrying the axe,
Came back, and laid his arm across
          her neck,
Her right arm winding round him. So they
          went . . .'
These lovely lines are from Sir Edward
          Arnold's translation.

And while we delight in reading those English translations of Sanskrit epics, we must be grateful to these early translators for making them accessible to the world. So that, as Thoreau said, 'the waters of the Ganges can flow in Walden Pond'.

Sounds of India . . .

The passing of a train.
The cries of station vendors.
The call of the peacock.
Dogs barking through the night.
The murmur of pigeons on the roof.
Drums in the distance.
Car horns in concert.
A flute player on a lonely hill.
A wedding band tunes up,
strikes up, passes down the road.
Children singing at the start of the school day.
Festival time, 'Holi hai!'
Mynas squabbling in a banyan tree.
Frogs in chorus on a rainy night.
Raindrops on old tin roofs.
Temple bells.
The call of the *muezzin*.
The roar of the crowd at a T-20 match.
A politician on a loudspeaker, asking for
your vote.
The hum of a passing plane.
The silence of the mountains.

THE COLOURS OF INDIA

No other country has so much colour . . .

Turbans of many colours.

Robes of many colours—orange, white,
yellow, pink.

Red sandstone forts, golden temples, palaces
embedded with *lapis-lazuli*, walls of amber,
tombs and monuments gleaming in the sun.

Marigolds everywhere. This is everyone's
flower—
in temples, in the home, at ceremonies.
Garlands of golden marigolds.

Birds of a myriad hues and colours . . .
Parrots in a mango tree.
Blue jays on the wind.
Peacocks strutting.
Kingfishers on fire.

Minivets, sunbirds, flycatchers, woodpeckers,
Kingfishers, all beautifully dressed.
As a boy, my father took me to the Gulf
of Kutch, and there I saw a beach
flooded with flamingoes, their glorious pink
transforming the sands into something
magical.

In the Sabzi-mandi, the fruit stalls
stand out because of their many coloured
offerings:
oranges from Nagpur, apples from the hills,
walnuts from Kashmir, pineapples from the
south, papayas from the north, mangoes,
guavas, grapes,
tomatoes from everywhere!

My walk through the busy market takes me
past the *halwai*, the little Sweet shop. I stop.
Impossible to pass it without sampling
something
from the colourful array of Indian sweets—
spangled golden jalebis, dripping gulab-
jamuns,
syrupy *ras-golas*, many-hued barfis and
halwas.
I help myself to a pink and white coconut
barfi. Enough, my friend! Don't overdo it.
Move on, move on . . .

Saris from Varanasi and Chennai
dazzle the onlooker.
Bangles from Jaipur. Is there no end to
colour?
There isn't. The front of a toy shop
is decorated with balloons. And a number
of
small children gather around a youth selling
candy floss. His pole is decorated with the
sugary pink sweet.

Where the bazaar ends there is an
old banyan tree, its many offshoots
providing shade
and shelter to beast and man. A labourer
is asleep beneath the tree, an
upturned basket forming a cushion for his
head. He has had a busy day.

There is money to be made in the
marketplace, but under the banyan tree
there is rest.

CAME THE VIRUS. . .

SOMETHING was missing during the past year and a half. It was the cheerful sight of children going to school—either walking to school in small towns and villages, or travelling in school buses to distant schools.

Most of them in smart uniforms, meeting
their friends, discussing the day ahead, and
what they would do in their holidays, after
the exams . . .

Exams! Our childhood, adolescence, teens,
seem to revolve around them.

And here they are, just back from nine months lockdown due this wretched COVID-19 virus which has spread around the globe, forcing us to wear masks and keep a safe distance from each other.

'We want to hold hands again!' So said a little girl to me the other day.

Our children are the future—the future of India and the world. They have ambitions, they want to grow up to be scientists, doctors, teachers, engineers, soldiers, seamen, pilots, writers, singers, actors, directors, farmers, astronauts, even politicians!

We must help them on their way. Give them
good schools, good teachers, good books,
the best of technology. We owe it to them.
We have made this world a difficult place
for them to grow up in.

Now we must rectify our mistakes, remove the boulders from the broken road, and create an atmosphere of tolerance and goodwill that will enable them to grow and develop in a world free of conflict.

Wrote Rabindranath Tagore: 'Every child comes with the message that god is not yet discouraged of man'.

So, give them the best of everything—playing-fields, libraries, lawns, nutritious food, open spaces for exercise, cheerful bright classrooms, gymnasiums, swimming pools—and one day they will bring honour to themselves and the country—and bundles of Olympic medals!

SOME of our boys and girls go into the Armed forces, and there could be no nobler choice than this.

We have long borders and envious neighbours. Mountain chains to the north and great coastal lines elsewhere are blessings, economically and geographically, but they need constant protection by land, sea and air.

The Indian Army has a great reputation. It has fought in two World Wars and many regional conflicts. Cadets from all over the world come to the Indian Military Academy for extensive and rigorous training.

Every regiment is proud of its history, its traditions and achievements, and their regimental histories make fascinating reading.

The character of the Indian Army, Navy and Air Force can be summed up thus: Courage, Discipline, Love for our nation. Which is why thousands from small towns and villages from all over the country converge on enlistment centres, to offer their services to the country.

MONUMENTS

Most visitors to India just see the Golden
Triangle—the monuments of Delhi,
Agra and Jaipur—forts, palaces,
ruined cities, tombs inlaid with marble,
graceful pavilions and gardens, all
monuments
to a glorious past.

Every town, every city in India, has monuments equally fascinating, but only the most venturesome visitors get to see them. We need to show off a little, and show our lesser-known treasures to the world.

But our greatest monument is not made of stone or marble. It is our Constitution, our Democracy. Only a few countries can boast of possessing such a treasure.

AND SO, we celebrate 75 years of Independence, of freedom from foreign rule.

We have many freedoms:
the freedom to build our own homes
the freedom to live wherever we wish to live
the freedom to travel
the freedom to read and write, and to speak freely
the freedom to take part in governance
the freedom to choose our own vocations.
We enjoy many freedoms.

But there are still a few that have yet to
be attained:

freedom from poverty and want
freedom from the shackles of the past
freedom from greed and envy
freedom from hate and fear.

The present is never our end. Past and present are means to an end. The future alone is our end. And striving for a better, greater future is our destiny.

ACKNOWLEDGEMENTS

My thanks to Premanka Goswami for
suggesting the theme of this little book.